A Book of Intercessions

For use in the Anglican Church at the Service of Holy
Communion on Sunday mornings

Keith Stonier

authorHOUSE

AuthorHouse™ UK
1663 Liberty Drive
Bloomington, IN 47403 USA
www.authorhouse.co.uk
Phone: UK TFN: 0800 0148641 (Toll Free inside the UK)
*   UK Local: (02) 0369 56322 (+44 20 3695 6322 from outside the UK)*

Published by AuthorHouse 11/03/2021

ISBN: 978-1-6655-9435-6 (sc)
ISBN: 978-1-6655-9436-3 (e)

Introduction

The word *intercession* has a number of meanings. In the broadest sense, it describes the process of interceding, or intervening, to an authority on behalf of others. The religious interpretation goes further as this relates to the actions of praying to God personally and as a spokesperson for other people. Prayers of *intercession* can address wide issues concerning the connection between the Almighty and believers. Also, the Intercessor may invite God to show His mercy in a more detailed way by citing a special need; for example, the plight of a person or group of people. The Intercessor appeals to God personally, in addition to occupying the intermediary position of praying as a representative of the congregation.

The intercessions in this book are designed to fulfil the requirements of the Anglican Church Year during the Sunday morning Holy Communion Service, together with some for special occasions. However, they can be adapted for other services. All have been tried and tested by being used in Church settings over a long period of time. The structure reflects the seasons of the Church Year, beginning with Advent. Two periods of 'ordinary time' are included. The first of these covers the anticipation of Lent and the second the full period of Trinity, ending with preparations for the time of Advent again.

With the exception of Holy Week, every section begins with a **template**; that is, a standard form for the prayers in that part of the book. Holy Week is treated as an exception by having only one Sunday morning Service (Palm Sunday), with no template required as Easter Sunday is included within the full season of Easter, following. Also, Intercessions for Christmas Eve, Christmas Day and Whit Sunday (Pentecost) are provided separately from the templates. All of the templates differ slightly from each other and have gaps in the text indicated by empty lines, where the Intercessor can insert topical pleas to God, for example concerning the problems of the world and the names of the sick and deceased. These are the items that help to define the unique character of the Intercessions offered by any one person.

This mark indicates the relevant places in the text where prayers can be inserted: *
Prayers are provided for this purpose at the end of each section. Intercessors can choose from these, adapt them at will or insert prayers of their own choice if they wish. Many of the prayers can be rotated and re-used over a cycle of weeks, especially those for the long season entitled, *ORDINARY TIME – Trinity & the Anticipation of Advent*. The prayers for special occasions include those for: Maundy Thursday, Good Friday, Mothering Sunday and Remembrance Sunday.

Some Intercessors may decide to use this book as a full or occasional resource over the cycle of the Church Year, while it is understood that others may prefer their own creative style to convey their messages. To those who choose to use this book, its value is intended to be the provision of a structure to aid the focusing of thoughts on things that really matter. This helps to render the Intercessor's prayers, *with* and *for* the congregation, as dedicated and meaningful as possible. There is no intention to place barriers, but to remove them and the book is offered with deep humility.

The author's permission is granted for the photocopying of any part of this book. Indeed, this is recommended, especially for the **templates**, to save time and avoid handwriting inside the book.

The Seasons of the Church Year

Advent (*arrival*)
… the beginning of the Church Year, including the first four Sundays

Christmas (*Christ's mass*)
… celebrating the birth of Jesus and his arrival among us (the 'Incarnation')

Epiphany (*sudden consciousness, understanding or manifestation*) …commemorating the visit of the Wise Men to Jesus and the revelation of this for all people

[Five weeks of 'ordinary time', anticipating Lent]

Lent
… a time of self-analysis, atonement, renunciation and personal study

Easter
…the death and resurrection of Jesus, including:
  the Feast of the Ascension (40th day of Easter) and
  the Day of Pentecost (50th day of Easter)

[Twenty-four weeks of Trinity and four weeks anticipating Advent]

Calendar of the Church Year

(Subject to variation, depending on the feast days that occur on Sundays)

ADVENT
The First Sunday of Advent
The Second Sunday of Advent
The Third Sunday of Advent
The Fourth Sunday of Advent
Christmas Eve

CHRISTMAS
Christmas Day
The First Sunday of Christmas
The Second Sunday of Christmas

EPIPHANY
(The Feast of the Epiphany, 6th January)
The First Sunday of Epiphany (The Baptism of Christ)
The Second Sunday of Epiphany
The Third Sunday of Epiphany
The Fourth Sunday of Epiphany
(The Presentation of Jesus in the Temple /Candlemas, 2nd February)

ORDINARY TIME – before Lent
The Fifth Sunday before Lent
The Fourth Sunday before Lent
The Third Sunday before Lent
The Second Sunday before Lent
The Sunday next before Lent

LENT
(Ash Wednesday)
The First Sunday of Lent
The Second Sunday of Lent
The Third Sunday of Lent
The Fourth Sunday of Lent (Mothering Sunday)
The Fifth Sunday of Lent (Passion Sunday)

HOLY WEEK
Palm Sunday
(Maundy Thursday)
(Good Friday)

EASTER
Easter Sunday
The Second Sunday of Easter
The Third Sunday of Easter
The Fourth Sunday of Easter
The Fifth Sunday of Easter
The Sixth Sunday of Easter
(Ascension Day)
The Seventh Sunday of Easter
Whit Sunday (Pentecost)

ORDINARY TIME – Trinity & the Anticipation of Advent
Trinity Sunday
The First Sunday after Trinity
The Second Sunday after Trinity
The Third Sunday after Trinity
The Fourth Sunday after Trinity
The Fifth Sunday after Trinity
The Sixth Sunday after Trinity
The Seventh Sunday after Trinity
The Eighth Sunday after Trinity
The Ninth Sunday after Trinity
The Tenth Sunday after Trinity
The Eleventh Sunday after Trinity
The Twelfth Sunday after Trinity
The Thirteenth Sunday after Trinity
The Fourteenth Sunday after Trinity
The Fifteenth Sunday after Trinity
The Sixteenth Sunday after Trinity   }
The Seventeenth Sunday after Trinity   } Harvest
The Eighteenth Sunday after Trinity   }
The Nineteenth Sunday after Trinity   } All Saints' Day / Sunday
The Twentieth Sunday after Trinity   } (1st November)
The Twenty-first Sunday after Trinity   }
The Last Sunday after Trinity   } Remembrance Sunday
The Fourth Sunday before Advent
The Third Sunday before Advent
The Second Sunday before Advent
The Sunday before Advent (Christ the King)

Prayerful Thoughts (Things to pray for)

1. To God, the Father Almighty we pray:
- that we may grow in understanding, faithfulness, love & respect for others
- that we can serve Your will and, in doing so, improve our world and help others to grow in their service & faithfulness
- that we are able to play a part in enhancing the lives of those around us, through Your mercy, the grace of our Lord Jesus Christ and the fellowship of the Holy Spirit
- for our families, our community, our country & nations of the world
- for improvement in our climate
- for Your blessing upon our friends and those we may dislike
- for those who are dear to us/close to our hearts and others known expressly to us who have problems in their lives, perhaps are experiencing great stress and are 'living in dark places' at present
- for people who are suffering the effects of ageing, especially those experiencing age-related disorders such as dementia
- for help for the poor
- for those who are unwell, their loved ones and the people who address their needs through social care and medical practice
- for those who have departed this life and their sorrowful loved ones
- for those who suffer violence and aggression, in their homes & throughout the world
- for the homeless, especially those living on the streets of big cities in the world
- for disaffected people who have lost their way, become susceptible to indoctrination, adopted strange beliefs and may have become persuaded to commit extreme acts of violence and terrorism … that they will return to ways of goodness, understanding and peace and cease planning to do harm
- for all who are suffering oppression in the countries of the world, especially people who are living under the threat of violence or the effects of extremism and may be enduring false imprisonment … also, for Christians being persecuted for their faith
- for Church leaders and the Church throughout the world
- for the poor, the sick & those requiring other forms of help … that their needs will be addressed in ways that are acceptable in Your sight, through the example of the ministry of Your Son Jesus Christ
- for leaders of nations, that they will act faithfully to perpetuate and enhance what is right in Your sight
- for medical practitioners and social care workers
- for improvements in world health, especially the elimination of disease.
Amen.

2. We offer our thanks for the good things that You have given to us, Lord, in Your wisdom: the beauty of our world, our joyful experiences, the sharing of love and respect between people, the development of learning powers, the growth of knowledge and healthy lifestyles, our families & friends and our freedom.
Amen.

Intercessions for ADVENT

The First Sunday of Advent
The Second Sunday of Advent
The Third Sunday of Advent
The Fourth Sunday of Advent
Christmas Eve (Morning Service or Midnight Mass)

Special Note:
Intercessions for **Christmas Eve** (Morning Service or Midnight Mass) are not included in the template. They are presented separately, at the end of this section of the book.

Template

For the _____ Sunday of ADVENT

1.   Dear Lord, on this _____ Sunday of Advent …

*

Lord in Your mercy, hear our prayer. Amen

2.   Dear Lord, we bring before You our concerns about the world in which we live:

_____

_____

_____

_____

_____

We ask, Lord …

*

Lord in Your mercy, hear our prayer. Amen

3.   Dear Lord, we pray for our local Church community, for Your Church throughout the world, for Church leaders and for our families and friends. (Also, we pray for the forthcoming marriage/s of _____ and that they will be blessed with much happiness).

Dear Lord …

*

Lord in Your mercy, hear our prayer. Amen

4. Dear Lord, we pray for all in sickness, pain or distress, for their loved ones and for those who help them:

_____

_____

_____

_____

[And,] Here is a quiet time for each one of us to pray for people known to us personally, who are in special need of the Lord's help. (pause)

*

Lord in Your mercy, hear our prayer. Amen.

5. Dear Lord, we pray for people who have passed on from this world and for their loved ones & friends.

[For:]

[And[In a time of quiet reflection we offer to You, Lord, our prayers for those known only to each one of us. (pause)

*

Lord in Your mercy, hear our prayer. Amen.

6. In our Closing Prayer we ask for the Lord's help to lead us forward in our lives,

*

May our prayers to You make a difference in our lives, help others and lead us closer to Your goodness and light.

Merciful Father, accept these prayers for the sake of Your son, our Saviour Jesus Christ. Amen.

Prayers to choose – for selection and inclusion in the template at the points marked:

*

1. … we seek Your help, at this beginning of a new Church Year, to refresh ourselves and find the time in our busy lives for quiet thought and reflection about Your great love for us and for the things in our lives that matter the most.

    … we ask for continued help, in our community and the world at large, with our preparations for the great celebration of the Lord's birth and the forthcoming Church Year.

    … we pray that You will grant that all who hear the Advent message will be refreshed in their relationship with You, more aware of Your presence in their lives and rejoice in the news of the coming of the Messiah.

    … we declare our trust in You to guide us. In the words of St. Paul: *We are Your children and ask for Your blessing to work for good. If You are for us, no-one can be against us.* [Words selected from Letter to the Romans (Chapter 8)]

2. … for peace in the world, especially for the victims of war and persecution, for the hurt and afflicted, for the poor, the lonely and the hungry and for any in special need at this time.

    … that You will be with Your people here on Earth:
    - who experience natural disasters
    - who are leaders and inspire them to work untiringly for peace, sustenance, shelter and healing for all, where there is suffering, pain and conflict [and] in the places where cruelty and unkindness can be found.

    Help us, Lord, to be touched by Your goodness and know the power of Your love.

    …for what we need … with great humility …and … thankful hearts. We know that Your peace will keep our hearts and minds safe in union with Christ Jesus [Words selected from Letter to the Philippians (Chapter 4)]

    … that the nations of the world will …*show their love by their tolerance towards others, their will to preserve unity and their efforts to build for a peace that binds us together.* [Words selected from Letter to the Ephesians (Chapter 4)]

3. … we pray, at this time of anticipation of the coming of Your Son Jesus, that all in our prayers will be blessed with compassion, concerned with things that really matter and continue to grow in faith.

… we know that … *Your kindness lasts for ever…* [Please] *…fulfil our needs so that we … [have] … what … is right … enough for good causes …* [and for those] *… in hardship.* [Words selected from Second Letter to the Corinthians (Chapter 9)]

4. Dear God, we ask for help for those who are unwell and for those who love and care for them, because we know that You are the great comforter and supporter of all who suffer and are in need.

Lord, please send Your gift of love to those who carry the burden of suffering for You have told us, through Paul, that *… love is patient, kind and eternal …* and that it supersedes even … *faith and hope.* Please help them with their burdens, through Your great love. [Words selected from First Letter to the Corinthians (Chapter 13)]

5. Dear God, we remember those who have come to You and ask that You will give comfort to their loved ones here on earth.

Our comfort is in You, Lord, for You have told us that You have a house in heaven for us … [and] …a home … [that You have made] … which lasts for ever. [Words selected from First Letter to the Corinthians (Chapters 15 and 16) and Second Letter to the Corinthians (Chapter 5)]

6. … please help and support us on our Advent journey.
When we are weak, grant us strength.
When we are troubled, speak to us with words of encouragement.
When we are fearful, give us the courage to do Your will.
Lift us with Your power and might.
Hold us close and lead us to do what is right and pleasing in Your sight.

… we ask for courage, strength and alertness in the face of our troubles so that we may do Your work with conviction and love. Please help us, in the words of St. Paul, … [to] *…carry our faith as a shield* … [through] *Your mighty power…*[and to] *… go as the Spirit leads us, for the benefit of all God's people … filling our minds with all that is good and deserving of Your praise.* [Words selected from First Letter to the Corinthians (Chapter 16), Letter to the Ephesians (Chapter 6) and Letter to the Philippians (Chapter 4)]

Intercessions for Christmas Eve
(Morning, Holy Communion Service **or** Midnight Mass)

<u>Introduction</u> You are invited to join-in, at the end of each prayer with the response:
We pray to the Lord. Amen.

1. Our prayers begin with silence as we take a quiet moment to hold in our hearts the people we love and who are special to us.

   (<u>pause</u>)

   Dear Lord Jesus, on this Eve of your birth as we remember how your light came into the world, open our hearts and minds to the message of Christmas-time: the coming of love into the world and what it should mean to each one of us.

   We pray to the Lord. Amen.

2. We continue by sharing our quiet thoughts with You, Lord, about the things that really matter to us and others. (pause) We pray especially for those who are going to find Christmas a time of sadness, stress or complexity.

   Lord Jesus, you were laid in a humble manger. Help our world to become a better, more loving and caring place. Have mercy on those who do not have our benefits and opportunities this Christmas time: the poor, the hungry, the oppressed, the homeless, the people in hospital and all who are separated from their loved ones. Help us to change anger and violence into peace and love. Lord Jesus, through your love revealed to all at Bethlehem, please help.

   We pray to the Lord. Amen

3. We think of the people who are in special need of the Lord's help at this time due to illness:

   Lord Jesus, before whom the humble shepherds worshipped and the Magi presented their gifts, please give comfort to those in special need and their loved ones, so that this Christmas-time is special for all of Your faithful people.

   We pray to the Lord. Amen.

4. We pray for all who have passed from this life and for their loved ones in their grief. Christmas is a time when the sorrow of loss is acute and meaningful.

Heavenly Father, we remember all who have come to You to enter into their new life with You and the great need of their loved ones for comfort.

We pray to the Lord. Amen.

5. We pray for our world and how we can play our part in making it greater and more beautiful through our understanding and continuation of God's love.

Lord Jesus, the obedience of Joseph & Mary, the joy of the angels and the wonder of the shepherds, remind us of the great mystery of this special time. Continue, we pray, to instil in us a profound sense of your abiding presence and the wonder of your love, that we may walk in God's ways and delight in His will. May the celebration of Your birth, Lord Jesus, be a signal for good things to happen.

We pray to the Lord. Amen.

6. Here is a Closing Prayer, in the form of a poem:

Come, Jesus most holy,
Enter our lives again.
Be our greatest gift,
And evermore remain.

We pray to the Lord. Amen.

Merciful Father …

Intercessions for CHRISTMAS

Christmas Day
The First Sunday of Christmas
The Second Sunday of Christmas

Intercessions for Christmas Day (Morning Service)

<u>Introduction</u> You are invited to join-in, at the end of each prayer with the response:
A great day has dawned upon us. Amen.

1. This is the birthday of Our Lord Jesus Christ. We thank You Almighty God for sending Your only Son into the world to renew our lives.
A great day has dawned upon us. Amen.

2. He was not born in a palace, but in the comparative poverty of a stable at the rear of an inn. When he grew up and began his ministry, the least and lowliest people in the world were of great importance to him. So, we pray for:
- people without homes
- people whose lives are in danger through warfare and disease
- those who work on this special day for the good of others
- those who are unemployed and long fo\r better times
[And, not least] – the sick and suffering, the lost and lonely, the deceased and their loved ones.

   O Lord Jesus, born to Mary and Joseph in a stable and sought by the Shepherds, we greet You with heartfelt happiness. We ask that all who are in need today will feel Your presence and be comforted through Your love.
A great day has dawned upon us. Amen.

3. We celebrate the birth of Jesus today, but e lives with us *always* (every day). We thank im for the blessings of safety, food, warmth and presents that we receive and we pray for families everywhere - especially mothers, their babies and children.

   O Lord Jesus, you lay in a manger, protected by Mary and Joseph and praised from on high by the Angels. We celebrate Your arrival with great joy and ask that families everywhere will find comfort in You – especially if they are separated and beset by difficulties.
A great day has dawned upon us. Amen.

4. In our final prayer, we ask You Lord Jesus that the peace, hope and goodwill we share on this special day of Your birth, will stay with us all year round.

   O Lord Jesus, help us to live and use our lives so that we spread the great message of Your everlasting love on this day and throughout the year.

   A great day has dawned upon us. Amen.

   Merciful Father …

Template

For the _____ Sunday of CHRISTMAS

<u>Introduction</u> You are invited to join-in, at the end of each prayer with the response,
   We pray to the Lord. Amen.

1.   We reflect on the coming of the light of Jesus into the world and ask that our hearts and minds will be opened to the special message of peace and goodwill that Christmas-tide brings.

                                        ✱

        We pray to the Lord. Amen.

2.   In our second prayer we address the needs of people for whom Christmas is a difficult time:
     - the lonely, housebound, oppressed and poor people of the world
     - the refugees, residing in countries away from their homelands

_____

_____

_____

_____

                                        ✱

        We pray to the Lord. Amen.

3.   We think of the people [from our list in Church / from the news media]/ [and those who are close to our own hearts] who are in need of the Lord's support:

_____

_____

_____

                                        ✱

We pray to the Lord. Amen.

4. Also, we pray for all who have passed from this life and for their loved ones in their sorrow. We think especially of:

_____

*

We pray to the Lord. Amen.

[And,] We pray for people who are dear to us and we see no more.

5. We think of our world and how we can play our part in making it greater and more beautiful through our recognition and continuation of God's love.

*

We pray to the Lord. Amen.

6. In our final prayer of Intercession, we thank God for sending His only Son to the world, for the bringing of joy into our hearts and the great offer of redemption He has made to us.

*

We pray to the Lord. Amen.

Merciful Father, accept these prayers for the sake of Your son, our Saviour Jesus Christ. Amen.

Prayers to choose – for inclusion in the template at the points marked:

*

1. Lord Jesus, help us to share the joy and peacefulness promised to us in the Christmas message. Please awaken the message of love in the hearts of people throughout the world.

    Lord Jesus, help us to appreciate the message of Your love and to play our part in spreading this through the coming year.

2. Lord Jesus, you were laid in a humble manger. Help our world to become a better, more loving and caring place for those who do not have our benefits and opportunities this Christmas time: the poor, the hungry, the oppressed, the homeless and all who are separated from their loved ones. Help our world to change the anger and violence of its wars and differences to peace and love. Lord Jesus, through Your love, revealed to the world at Bethlehem, please hear our words.

    Our prayer to You, O Lord,
    Is one of joy and hope,
    For peace throughout the world
    With great and wondrous scope.

3. Lord Jesus, before whom the humble shepherds worshipped and the Magi presented their gifts, please give comfort to those in special need and their loved ones, so that this Christmas-time is special for all of Your faithful people.

    Lord Jesus, we pray for all who suffer and their loved ones and ask that you will tend them with your loving goodness.

4. Lord Jesus, please receive all who have come to you at this time to enter into their new life with you and please give comfort to their loved ones.

    Lord Jesus, we pray for the deceased. We thank you for their earthly lives, their uplifting into your presence and the brightness of their new lives with you. We ask, also, that their loved ones will receive your healing power to ease their grief and sorrow.

5. Lord Jesus, the obedience of Joseph & Mary, the joy of the angels and the wonder of the shepherds, remind us of the great mystery of this holy time. We pray that you will continue to instil in us a profound sense of your abiding presence and the wonder of your love, so that we walk in your ways and know your will. May this season of Christmas-tide be a time of good will that continues for the rest of the year.

O God, You sent Your Son Jesus into the world to save us through forgiveness, hope in the future and love for the unloved. We ask for Your blessing on us as we seek to reflect that message in our lives.

6. The greatest Christmas gift of all
Was never placed beneath a tree,
But lay within a manger
Beneath a star, for all to see.

Enter our hearts, Lord Jesus,
Joyful let us be.
Fill us with a goodness,
Clear for all to see.

Merciful Father ...

Intercessions for EPIPHANY

The First Sunday of Epiphany
- The Baptism of Christ

The Second Sunday of Epiphany

The Third Sunday of Epiphany

The Fourth Sunday of Epiphany
- The Presentation of Jesus in the Temple / Candlemas
(The accepted date of this special event is 2nd February,
but the Fourth Sunday of Epiphany is when it is celebrated.)

Special Note:
Unique prayers for **The Baptism of Christ** and **The Presentation of Jesus in the Temple /
Candlemas** are located in the **Prayers** at the end of this section of the book.

Template

For the _____ Sunday of EPIPHANY

1. Heavenly Father, we offer our prayers to You, in hope of Your great mercy and seek the light of Your goodness.

   *

   Lord in Your mercy, hear our prayer. Amen

2. Heavenly Father, our world is in great need of Your help:

   _____

   _____

   _____

   _____

   *

   Lord in Your mercy, hear our prayer. Amen

3. Our Great Redeemer, we offer a prayer to You that addresses our hopes for our local Churches, for people of faith throughout the world and for those who are on a journey of searching for You. (In addition, we pray for _____, whose banns of marriage have been announced today, at this joyful time in their lives).

   *

   Lord in Your mercy, hear our prayer. Amen

4. Gracious Lord, we bring before You the names of all who are known to us who are unwell at this time. Their need for Your comfort and reassurance is uppermost in our thoughts. We pray for the people who love and care for them. Also, we pray for all, throughout the world, who are unwell and we hold in our silent thoughts those who are special and known only to each one of us.

_____

_____

_____

_____

*

Lord in Your mercy, hear our prayer. Amen.

5. Almighty Father, we pray for those who have departed this life recently and for their families and friends.

[We name, especially:] _____

Also, we reflect silently about the departed who are beloved by each one of us.

*

Lord in Your mercy, hear our prayer. Amen.

6. O Lord our Heavenly Father, we give thanks to You for the shining presence of Your Son Jesus in our lives at this Epiphany-time. We ask that our prayers will bring us closer to his goodness and that his light will shine on those for whom we pray.

*

Merciful Father, accept these prayers for the sake of Your son, our Saviour Jesus Christ. Amen.

Prayers to choose – for inclusion in the template at the points marked:

＊

1. Heavenly Father, as the star led the Wise men to the Infant Jesus, may the radiance of Your presence lead us and light our path. Help us to come before You as people of Your light.

   Lord, we ask You to help us, in our turbulent world, to find hope, comfort and the peace of mind that come with the knowledge of Your presence among us.

   Heavenly Father, we come before You with our cares about the world, hopes for the future and private thoughts to share with You.
   > We look to You in humility
   > We search for You in prayer
   > Breathe Your spirit on us
   > Grant to us Your care.

   [The Baptism of Christ] Heavenly Father, we give thanks for the baptism of Your Son Jesus. We ask that this special celebration of love will inspire us to wash away doubts and anticipate the prospect of new beginnings.

   [The Presentation of Jesus in the Temple / Candlemas] Heavenly Father, as we celebrate the day when Jesus was presented in the Temple, we present ourselves to You. We ask that goodness will live in our hearts and that the prospect of fresh beginnings will inspire us.

2. O Lord, when the Wise Men came to Your Son, Jesus, they paid homage to him as a king and acknowledged that his birth was a revelation of Your love for mankind. May we follow in his footsteps and seek for goodness and peace.

   Dear Lord, please help us to follow the star that leads to peace, love and justice and away from unrest and strife. We pray for all who are displaced, homeless and hurt by the troubles of the world. Also, we pray for the leaders of nations, that they will follow paths of goodness.

   Lord, we ask that You will pour out the living water of Your Spirit upon our world and all the needs of its nations and people.

   Heavenly Father, we pray for this world and its need for Your light:
   - for the people who bear the responsibilities of government that they will respond to You in their search for justice and peace
   - for the people of every nation that they will obtain freedom from oppression

- for people in the world who are indoctrinated with hate, that they will abandon evil, misguided thoughts and practices and direct their lives to what is good.

Heavenly Father, please continue to watch over Your people with tender love and compassion.

3. O Lord, we pray for all involved in our Church and local community groups and in the Church throughout the world, that they will continue to be encouraged and influenced by Your guiding light.

Heavenly Father, please help all involved in our Church, local community and Churches throughout the world to serve under the influence of Your guiding light.

4. *Lord, please send Your love into the hearts of all who suffer, that they will receive the blessings of joy, peace and hope.* [Words selected from Letter to the Romans (Chapters 5 and 15)]

Heavenly Father, please help those who suffer and those who care for them to know that the presence of Your guiding light is with them always. Please bring the comfort of Your peace and healing to them, so that their needs are met in You.

5. Lord, we pray for the departed and their fulfilment in You. Also, we pray that the burden of grief of their loved ones will be lifted through the comfort that You give so freely.

Heavenly Father, we pray for all who have come to You at this time, into their new life, and for the consolation of their loved ones.

6. Let our prayers to You, Lord, guide us in our lives, lead us to know how to love others and give us hope for the future.
>> Come into our hearts
>> Enter our lives anew
>> Be the central part
>> Of all (that) we say and do.

We are mindful of Your presence, Lord, and seek Your help in our prayers to do what is right and to walk in Your ways, especially through the teachings and example of Your Son, Jesus. We invite You to be a light in our lives and to lead us towards hope, peace and goodness

Thank You, Lord, for receiving our prayers. We know that they do not go unheeded and that Your love for us never fails. Please refresh us, equip us to be Your faithful servants and help us to make a positive difference in our lives and the lives of others.

Merciful Father …

Intercessions for ORDINARY TIME – before LENT

The Fifth Sunday before Lent
The Fourth Sunday before Lent
The Third Sunday before Lent
The Second Sunday before Lent
The Sunday next before Lent

Template (Ordinary Time – before LENT)

For the _____ Sunday (or Sunday next) before LENT

1. O Lord God,

   *

   Lord in Your mercy, hear our prayer. Amen

2. O Lord God, we bring before You our prayers for the people of the world:

   - our cares about_____

   - our concern for_____

   - our worries about_____

   - our wish for_____

   - our thanks for_____

   *

   Lord in Your mercy, hear our prayer. Amen

3. O Lord God, we pray for the Christian Church throughout the world and its people: the faithful witnesses of Your great love who attend Church frequently and those who profess the faith, but do not or cannot practise their faith regularly owing to their perceptions, the pressures of the world or for other reasons. We pray especially for people who are suffering for their faith, often in distant lands and living under the threat of harsh, unsympathetic regimes.

   (Also, we pray for the forthcoming marriage/s of ……………………………….. and for their happiness and fulfilment in married life.)

   *

   Lord in Your mercy, hear our prayer. Amen

4.　O Lord God, we pray for all in sickness, pain or distress, their loved ones and all who help them. In particular, we think of:

- _____

- _____

- _____

- _____

[And,] We call to mind the people known only to each one of us who are in need of the relief and tranquillity that come from You, Lord.

✱

Lord in Your mercy, hear our prayer. Amen.

5.　O Lord God, we pray for people who have passed on from this world and for their loved ones & friends.

[For:] _____ .

[And] Please take a short time, now, to pray for people dear to your hearts.

✱

Lord in Your mercy, hear our prayer. Amen.

6.　In our final prayer we ask, O Lord God, for the pouring of Your blessing upon us according to our needs: support for the faithful to live and work in Your name, spiritual succour for those in need of a renewal of their faith, help for the poor, comfort for the sorrowful and the reassurance that only You can give for those who are oppressed and persecuted.

✱

Merciful Father, accept these prayers for the sake of your son, our Saviour Jesus Christ. Amen.

Prayers to choose – for inclusion in the template at the points marked:

*

1. .… on our progress towards Lent we ask for Your continuing help in our preparations, to allow us to reflect on what matters most in our lives and on the immensity of Your love for us.

   … we place ourselves in Your presence with our personal thoughts and shared supplications.

   … we are in awe of Your greatness, thank You for the good things in our lives and bring our contemplations before You.

   … we seek Your guidance in our reflections on ourselves, our relationship with You and the nature of our world.

   … we look towards the season of Lent with anticipation that You will guide us on a journey through our innermost thoughts about ourselves, our service and our awareness that nothing is outside Your love.

2. O Lord God, we pray for the people and nations in great need of You at this time. We ask for help for them so that they are comforted and supported by Your everlasting, faithful presence.

   O Lord God, we ask for spiritual sustenance for the people in our prayers today. Please help them to feel reassured and renewed in their hopefulness by Your presence.

   We trust in You, Lord. In the words of Psalm 46: **[You are] … *our shelter and strength, always ready to help in times of trouble. So, we will not be afraid, even if the earth is shaken and mountains fall into the ocean depths, even if the seas roar and rage and the hills are shaken by the violence. The Lord Almighty is with us, supreme among the nations, supreme over the world.***"

3. O Lord God, we pray for Christian people throughout the world, who worship in diverse ways and many different places, and a Church that accommodates all of their needs and differences.

   O Lord God, we know that the turning of people to You is a time of great rejoicing in Heaven. We pray for the reaching out of the Church inclusively, to people with so many needs and in different circumstances.

4. O Lord God, we ask for help for those who suffer and for those who care for them and, especially, that You will comfort and support them in their time of need.

O Lord God, please help all who suffer, the loved ones who sustain them and the dedicated people who help them and that they will know of Your loving presence in their lives.

5. O Lord God, we remember those who have come to You and ask that You will give comfort to their loved ones here on earth.

O Lord, we thank You for the life of every person who has gone from us and has come to You, to share in everlasting life with You. We pray for them and for their loved ones.

6. O Lord God, we give thanks for Your great gifts to us. We ask, with good hearts and mindful of Your loving mercy, that we can understand and follow Your will for us and that we can reflect the loving, peaceful, caring ways of Your Son, our Saviour Jesus Christ.

O Lord God, we ask for a peaceful, loving, caring world that is more aware of its environment and pleasing in Your sight.

In the words of Psalm 67:
God be merciful to us and bless us; look on us with kindness... [so that] ***... the whole world may know Your will ...*** [and] ***... all nations may know Your salvation.***

Merciful Father ...

Intercessions for LENT

(Ash Wednesday)
The First Sunday of Lent
The Second Sunday of Lent
The Third Sunday of Lent
The Fourth Sunday of Lent *(Mothering Sunday)*
The Fifth Sunday of Lent (Beginning of Passiontide)

Special Note:
Unique prayers for **Mothering Sunday** and **Passion Sunday** are located in the **Prayers** at the end of this section of the book.

Template

For the _____ Sunday of LENT

1. During this season of Lent we ask the Lord to increase our understanding of His message of love for us, what this means in our lives and how we can grow in our faith.

   *

   Lord in Your mercy, hear our prayer. Amen

2. Dear Lord, we bring before You our anxiety about the world and expectations for its future:

   - our cares for _____

   - our worries about _____

   - our hopes for _____

   - our concern about _____

   - we think, especially, of _____

   *

   Lord in Your mercy, hear our prayer. Amen

3. Dear Lord, we pray for Christians who are persecuted for their faith, Your Church in the world, Church leaders, the Churches in our Diocese, the dedicated organisers of community clubs and our families and our friends.

   (Also, we pray for the forthcoming marriage/s of …………………………...……..
   and that they will be blessed with much happiness).

   *

   Lord in Your mercy, hear our prayer. Amen

4. Dear Lord, we pray for all in sickness, pain or distress and for their loved ones and carers.

[From our list in Church we pray for:] _____

_____

_____

[And, we hold in our thoughts those who are known to us personally.]

Lord in Your mercy, hear our prayer. Amen.

5. Dear Lord, we pray for people who have passed on from this world to come to Your holy place and for their loved ones. We remember, in our prayers today:

_____

[And, we express our silent prayers for those who are known to us personally.]

*

Lord in Your mercy, hear our prayer. Amen.

6. Dear Lord, we thank You for listening to our prayers and for the greatness of the world You have given us to be our responsibility.

Through You, Lord, may our prayers help us in our lives and improve the lives of others so that we reach ever closer to Your goodness and light.

*

Merciful Father, accept these prayers for the sake of Your son, our Saviour Jesus Christ. Amen.

Prayers to choose – for inclusion in the template at the points marked

*

1. Lord Jesus, help us to seek you, find you and enrich our awareness of the radiance of your love.

   Lord Jesus, we ask you to help us face temptation as you did in the wilderness. Turn us away from greed, unkindness, cruelty, intolerance and the many other inducements to transgress found in the modern world. Help us to find and be surrounded by your love.

   Lord Jesus, breathe your spirit upon us and guide us towards the Father's everlasting love as we remember the words that you spoke, 'not our will, but your will be done'.

   [Mothering Sunday] Dear Lord, on this Mothering Sunday we pray for Mothers everywhere and their importance in homes and families. We pray for our own Mothers, whether they are with us every day, living far away from us or we see them no more. We pray for Mothers who have been separated from their children, perhaps through social circumstances, imprisonment, injustice or warfare, and long to be with them again. We pray for Mothers who have lost their children and for Mothers who find the tasks of motherhood a great challenge. We pray for women everywhere who long to be Mothers. Lastly, we pray for all who give love and show compassion in their caring for others just as if they are Mothers. We thank You, Lord, for the unconditional love that Mothers give in such great abundance and we are sure in the knowledge that this reflects the unconditional love that You have for us.

   [Passion Sunday]
   Introduction We reflect, in our prayers today, on the passion of Jesus Christ. We think about his love for us and the giving of his life for our salvation.
   Prayer
   Dear Lord Jesus, we recognise, accept and thank you gratefully for the love that you show to us. We ask to repay that love by means of what we do for others, by putting their needs before our own in our prayers and in whatever practical ways that we can manage. You gave your life, Lord Jesus, for our salvation. We ask that those who lead the nations will be mindful of the debt of gratitude that is owed to you, that they will act with grace, patience and inner strength and do their utmost to bring peace and reconciliation to the world.

2. Dear God, we ask that You will pour out the living water of Your Spirit upon our world and the needs of its nations and people. Help us to find refreshment, hope and comfort in You and the peace of mind that comes with the knowledge of Your presence among us.

We seek the Lord's help for those in our prayers with words chosen from the Psalms: *In times of trouble … [we] … pray to the Lord* (Psalm 77). *Listen to … [our] … words, O Lord, and hear … [our] … sighs* (Psalm 5). *You, Lord, are all … [we] … have … [our] future is in Your hands* (Psalm 16). *Let … [our] … cry for help reach You, Lord* (Psalm 119).

3. Dear Lord, we thank You for the talents and endeavours of those who work so hard for the benefit of others in the true spirit of Christianity.

We ask this, Lord in the words of the Psalms: *Remember, O Lord, …* [Your] *… tender mercies and … loving kindness …* [towards us] *… they have been ever of old,* (Psalm 25) *… For as the heaven is high … so great is …* [Your] *… mercy,* (Psalm 103) *… O Lord, … let …* [Your[*… loving kindness and … truth … preserve* [us], (Psalm 40).

4. Dear God, we ask for help for those who suffer and for those who care for them. Breathe Your spirit upon them, to comfort and support them in their time of need.

We trust in You, Lord, to help in our time of need. In the words of Psalm 103: *The Lord is merciful and loving … As a father is kind to his children, so the Lord is kind to those who honour Him … His love lasts for ever and His goodness endures for all generations …*

5. Dear God, please breathe Your spirit on those who have come to You and give comfort to their loved ones here on earth.

We trust in You, Lord. In the words of Psalm 23: *The Lord is my shepherd … He lets me rest … and leads me to quiet pools of fresh water … I know that [His] … goodness and love will be with me all my life and [His] ... house will be my home [forever].*

6. At this special time of Lent, we reflect on the meaning of transgression, the redeeming power of Your love and the support given to us through Your holy word. If we disappoint and fall, raise us up to do what is right and turn us around with Your unfailing love so that we continue to follow Your living word.

In the words of the Psalms:
Whoever goes to the Lord for safety, whoever remains under the protection of the Almighty, can say to Him, "You are my defender. You are my God. In You I trust." (Psalm 91) *Your kingdom is founded on righteousness and justice; love and faithfulness are shown in all You do.* (Psalm 89) *Bring us back, Lord God Almighty…[and]…show us Your mercy.* (Psalm 80)

Merciful Father …

Intercessions for HOLY WEEK

Palm Sunday
Maundy Thursday
Good Friday

Intercessions for Palm Sunday (Morning Service)

Introduction

Let us pray. You are invited to join in with the words, **Be with us in our lives, Lord Jesus** at the end of each prayer.

1. We bring to You, God the Father, our reflections about the events of Holy Week and their meaning for us in our lives. The story that began with betrayal, fear, persecution and crucifixion ended with the vision of a new life with You. We thank You for the power of Your Son, Jesus, in our lives today.
Be with us in our lives, Lord Jesus, Amen

2. Jesus washed the feet of his disciples. He put others before himself and revealed the goodness of serving. Help us, God the Father, to serve others, put their needs first, do what we can to alleviate suffering and look for positives in life.
Be with us in our lives, Lord Jesus, Amen

3. Jesus prayed while his disciples were sleeping. Help us, God the Father, to know and use the power of prayer and to have a prayerful dialogue with You that enables us to understand what is right and acceptable in Your sight. We address this prayer to God the Father for people who are unwell, lonely, dispossessed, frightened and for those who have passed on recently to another life.
Be with us in our lives, Lord Jesus, Amen

4. Jesus was betrayed by Judas. There are times when we may feel hurt, abandoned or misunderstood. Help us, God the Father, to forgive. to wipe away any resentment and avoid hurting others.
Be with us in our lives, Lord Jesus, Amen

5. Jesus was subjected to a false trial, the severe punishment of flogging and to crucifixion. God the Father, we ask that You will help all who suffer oppression and that You will be their comfort through the troubles of injustice, persecution, darkness and separation. Also, we pray that You will be with their loved ones who suffer the pain in almost equal measure.
Be with us in our lives, Lord Jesus, Amen

6. Jesus forgave all who mistreated him. They showed no pity, but he asked for forgiveness for them, because they did not understand the wrong that they were doing. His love was limitless and unconditional. We ask, Lord Jesus, that all who search for forgiveness through you, and this includes ourselves, will find it and transform it into goodness.
Be with us in our lives, Lord Jesus, Amen

Merciful Father, accept these prayers for the sake of Your son, our Saviour Jesus Christ. Amen.

A Prayer for Maundy Thursday

You made yourself a servant, Lord Jesus, in the washing of feet and celebrated the sharing of bread and wine as a lasting memory of Your presence among us. You prayed in the full knowledge of what was to come and what you must do in order to fulfil your work in the world. Your compassion and sacrifice are lasting examples for us when we face the problems of our own lives and of the world.

We thank you, Lord Jesus. Amen.

A Prayer for Good Friday

Lord Jesus, you suffered abuse, terrible punishment and hung on a cross for us. You sought forgiveness for those who persecuted you. You did all of this for our salvation.

We thank you, Lord Jesus.

Intercessions for EASTER

Easter Sunday

The Second Sunday of Easter

The Third Sunday of Easter

The Fourth Sunday of Easter

The Fifth Sunday of Easter

The Sixth Sunday of Easter

(Ascension Day)

The Seventh Sunday of Easter

Whit Sunday (Pentecost)

Special Note:
The end of the **Prayers** section contains two items for **Ascension Day**. These are followed by
Intercessions for Whit Sunday / Pentecost.

Template

For the _____ Sunday of EASTER

1. The weeks of Easter and Pentecost are looked upon as the most important in the Church's Year, because they reveal a story to us of transformation through the death, transfiguration and ascension of our Lord Jesus Christ. So, in our first prayer, we welcome the transforming power of this message into our lives.

*

Lord in Your mercy, hear our prayer. Amen

2. We thank You, Lord, for the good things in our lives: for the beauty of the changing seasons, the friendship of others and the dedication of so many to Your service. We know that the world is in great need of Your continuing help and we pray for :

_____

_____

_____

_____

*

Lord in Your mercy, hear our prayer. Amen

3. We ask for the Lord's help for all who are unwell and for their loved ones. We give thanks for the dedicated people who address the health and social care of others and, in our silent prayers, we think of those who are close to our hearts and in need of the Lord's blessing. [For:]

_____

_____

_____

_____

*

Lord in Your mercy, hear our prayer. Amen

4. We pray for people who have passed-on from their earthy life and for their loved ones. [For:]

_____

[And,] We offer our silent prayers for those held in our hearts.

*

Lord in Your mercy, hear our prayer. Amen.

5. Jesus suffered on the cross for us and there are many who suffer in the world, today. Here is a special prayer for persecuted and oppressed people throughout the world, who are experiencing the anguish of injustice:

*

Lord in Your mercy, hear our prayer. Amen.

6. We pray for the use of God's gifts in this Church, our community and the world. We think of our Church family, the congregation here today, our spiritual leaders and the work of the Church in places where worship is difficult. Also, we pray for all who teach and are taught in schools and other places of education.

[(And,) We pray for ……………………………………. and for their happiness in their forthcoming marriage/s].

*

Lord in Your mercy, hear our prayer. Amen.

7. Lord, help us to repay Your trust and great mercy towards us. Thank You for the beauty of Your creation. Help us to use the gifts You have given us wisely, to carry forward Your word and to be messengers of Your great love, especially as it is expressed through the risen Lord Jesus. We ask for Your help, Lord, in passing on to future generations a good, caring and loving world and we look for the growth of Your kingdom in the world.

We hope in You, Lord, and thank You for listening to our prayers and innermost thoughts.

*

Merciful Father, accept these prayers for the sake of Your son, our Saviour Jesus Christ. Amen.

Prayers to choose – for inclusion in the template at the points marked

*

1. We offer our shared and private prayers to You, Lord, and ask to use the example of the Easter story for good in our lives.

   Lord, help us to be advocates of Your great love this Easter-time through our concern for those in need and our appreciation of the positive things in life that we can use to build for the future.

   Lord, we ask You to strengthen us to become messengers of Your word and enlighten us so that healing and forgiveness are known to us through Your unending love.

   We respond in our prayers, Lord, to the events of Easter-time and ask to be emissaries of Your sacrifice and love. We ask to be understanding of need and generous with the help we give to others.

   Help us, Lord, by means of the messages of sacrifice and compassion in the Easter story, to be guided (and to guide others) through the darkest places and difficult times of life, and lead us ever closer to Your everlasting Kingdom.

   As we receive the message of the Easter story and offer our shared and private prayers to You, Lord, send Your Holy Spirit to us and surround us with Your love.

   In the words of the Psalms: *[Our] … help will come from the Lord, who made heaven and earth … [Our] protector is always awake…[He] is by…[our]…side to protect…[us]* (Psalm 121). *The Lord Almighty is with us, supreme among the nations, supreme over the world* (Psalm 46).

2. We ask for a more peaceful, loving and caring world for all of Your people, especially those who have lost dignity and hope in their lives. Show us, Lord, how we can play our part in knowing how and when to help so that our world is better for everyone.

   Lord, we pray for all of Your people, particularly those who feel that they have been downgraded and rejected in life. We ask for their renewal through You and promise not to ignore their plight. We seek to play our part in bringing about good changes in the world.

   Our hope is in You, Lord. In the words of John's First Letter and Psalm 67: *God is love … [and] … there is no fear in love … Perfect love drives out all fear* (I John, 4: vs. 16 & 18). *God be merciful to us and … look on us with kindness … so that all nations may know Your salvation* (Psalm 67).

3. Dear Lord, we ask for help for those who suffer, especially for their support, comfort and reassurance in their time of need. Also, we pray for their loved ones and for those who care for them in hospitals and the community,

Our hope is in You, Lord, for Your help in time of need. In the words of St. Paul's Letter to the Romans and Psalm 39: *We know that in all things God works for good with those who love Him* (Romans 8: v. 28) *Hear…[our]… prayer, Lord, and…come to…[our]…aid…* (Psalm 39).

4. O Lord, we thank You for the life of every person who has gone from us and has come to You, and we pray for their loved ones here on earth.

Our hope is in You, Lord. In the words of the Psalms: *… the Lord has promised his blessing…[for]… life that never ends* (Psalm 133}. *[His] … house will be … [our]… home … [forever]* (Psalm 23).

5. Please send Your great gift of love, Lord, to the people in this world who are carrying the burdens of injustice and oppression. Help them to bear those burdens with faith, dignity and renewed hope for the future, in the full knowledge that You are with them.

These words of comfort are selected from the Psalms: *In times of trouble … [we] … pray to the Lord* (Psalm 77). *[Our] future is in Your hands* (Psalm 16). *Let … [our] … cry for help reach You, Lord* (Psalm 119).

6. Lord, make us one in heart and mind, as we participate in and serve our community. Make our service kind, true and loving. Make the products and effects of our service good and pleasing in Your sight.

In the words of The Book of Job and Psalm 80: *God alone knows the way … [He] sees the ends of the earth … [and]… everything under the sky* (Job 28, vs. 23-24). *Lord God Almighty … show us Your mercy* (Psalm 80).

7. Dear God, help us to repay Your trust in us and Your great mercy towards us. Give us understanding of how we can carry forward Your word and, through this, to be messengers of Your great love for the world. Grant us the will and the means to pass on to future generations a good world, that is acceptable in Your sight.

Lord, we hope in You and thank You for listening to our prayers and innermost thoughts.

Merciful Father …

Prayers for Ascension Day (or for adapting to the nearest Sunday)

We give praise for your Ascension, Lord Jesus, and direct our thoughts to your heavenly kingdom. We seek your guidance in our lives so that, in the fullness of time, we may follow you to the place where you have gone.

At this time of your Ascension, Lord Jesus, we share with you the driving away of all fears and our hopes for a new life with you. Equip us to be instruments of your peace and love in this world and furnish us with the wonder of your everlasting presence in our lives.

Merciful Father ...

Intercessions for Whit Sunday / Pentecost (Morning Service)

1. Let us pray
   On this Pentecost Sunday, we rejoice in the presence of God through the Holy Spirit and ask for help with our lives and the lives of others. Uppermost in our minds are the difficulties faced by people in our world and we offer our list of concerns and our private thoughts to the Lord God:
   - We know that there are many people whose faith has to carry them through ordeals and torments. We ask, O God through the Holy Spirit, for help for them and enlightenment in the places around the world where this is happening.
   - We pray for people who are caught up in the effects of unrest and war and that peace and love will come soon, to replace suffering, destruction and persecution.
   - We pray for people experiencing the problems of divided nations and that You, O God through the Holy Spirit, will enlighten their leaders so that differences are resolved.
   - We pray for the people in our own society and in other nations who have forgotten the ways of peace and love, especially those who hold violent, angry beliefs that cause them to behave in antagonistic and socially unacceptable ways
   - We pray for people who feel that society is against them or has rejected them, especially the homeless, those in prison and those living in a variety of forms of care.

- O God through the Holy Spirit, we pray for Your love and support for all who are suffering through severe illness and ageing difficulties and for their families.
- We pray for people of faith throughout the world.
- We pray for people everywhere who are seeking the living God in their lives.

O God in three persons, please help those for whom we pray, that they will obtain the blessings of peace, unity and harmony through You. We pray to receive the joy of living our lives in ways that are acceptable in Your sight. May the union of life in the Trinity be a model for us and reveal the importance of a deeper union with You.

Lord, in Your mercy, hear our prayer. Amen

2. In our prayers, we remember those known to us personally and from the community who are ill or troubled and for those who care for them. In particular, we think of:

_____

_____

_____

_____

Also, we thank You, O God through the Holy Spirit, for the dedicated people in the care and health sectors, whose work is a revelation of love. Lord, please help all who suffer, those who endure with them and those who help them to be filled with the life of the Trinity and experience Your loving help.

Lord in Your mercy, hear our prayer. Amen.

3. We pray for those who have passed-on from their earthy lives, for their loved ones and for the people who are recalled by each one of us in our private thoughts. [For:]

_____.

O Lord, we thank You for the life of every person who is gone from us and has come to You, to share the life of the Trinity forever. We pray for them and for their loved ones.

Lord, in Your mercy, hear our prayer. Amen.

4. We pray for the use of God's gifts in this Church and community: for Churches everywhere and for their leaders.

[Also, we pray for ………………………………….. and for much happiness in their forthcoming marriage/s].

Lord, we praise You for revealing to us the mystery of the Trinity. Help us to grow in faithfulness and may our prayers and service be pleasing in Your sight.

Lord, in Your mercy, hear our prayer. Amen.

5. We thank You, Lord, for listening to our prayers on this special day.

Merciful Father, accept these prayers for the sake of Your son, our Saviour Jesus Christ. Amen.

Intercessions for ORDINARY TIME
- Trinity & the Anticipation of Advent

Trinity Sunday
The First Sunday after Trinity
The Second Sunday after Trinity
The Third Sunday after Trinity
The Fourth Sunday after Trinity
The Fifth Sunday after Trinity
The Sixth Sunday after Trinity
The Seventh Sunday after Trinity
The Eighth Sunday after Trinity
The Ninth Sunday after Trinity
The Tenth Sunday after Trinity
The Eleventh Sunday after Trinity
The Twelfth Sunday after Trinity
The Thirteenth Sunday after Trinity
The Fourteenth Sunday after Trinity
The Fourteenth Sunday after Trinity
The Fifteenth Sunday after Trinity
The Sixteenth Sunday after Trinity   }
The Seventeenth Sunday after Trinity   } Harvest
The Eighteenth Sunday after Trinity   }
The Nineteenth Sunday after Trinity   } All Saints' Day / Sunday
The Twentieth Sunday after Trinity   } (1st November)
The Twenty-first Sunday after Trinity   }
The Last Sunday after Trinity   } Remembrance Sunday
The Fourth Sunday before Advent
The Third Sunday before Advent
The Second Sunday before Advent
The Sunday before Advent (Christ the King)

Special Note:
Unique prayers for **Trinity Sunday**, **Harvest**, **All Saints' Day** and **Remembrance Sunday** are located in the **Prayers** at the end of this section of the book.

Template (Ordinary Time – Trinity)

For: **Trinity Sunday**

or

The _____ Sunday after Trinity

or

All Saints' Day / All Saints' Sunday

or

The _____ Sunday before Advent

or

The Sunday before Advent

1. We offer our prayers to You, our eternal, ever-loving Father, in awe of Your merciful goodness.

    *

    Lord in Your mercy, hear our prayer. Amen

2. Lord, our thoughts reach out to the troubles of the world in which we live and to people who are in great need of Your presence. [To:]

    _____

    _____

    _____

    *

    Lord in Your mercy, hear our prayer. Amen

3. We pray for people known to us and throughout the world who are unwell and for those who are close to them through the ties of love and caring. Also, we hold in our silent thoughts and prayers those who are special to us. [We pray for:]

    _____

    _____

    *

    Lord in Your mercy, hear our prayer. Amen

4. We pray for those who have finished their earthy lives, for the loved ones who miss them so much and we hold in our silent thoughts those who have gone from us and are close to our hearts.

[From our list in Church, we pray for:] _____

*

Lord in Your mercy, hear our prayer. Amen.

5. We pray for the spiritual leaders and people of faith in this Church and other Christian communities throughout the world and for Christians who face the threat of persecution for their beliefs.

(Also,) We pray to You, Lord, for people involved in baptism and marriage celebrations: [For:] ……………………………………....…….. - and for happiness and fulfilment in their lives together.

*

Lord in Your mercy, hear our prayer. Amen.

6. Dear Lord, we thank You for listening to our prayers to You, through which we have expressed our concerns (about our world) and our hopes (for the future). We are grateful for the love You give and we trust in You to show us how we can achieve goodness and live acceptably in Your sight.

*

May our prayers to You make a difference in our lives, in the lives of others and lead us closer to You.

Merciful Father, accept these prayers for the sake of Your son, our Saviour Jesus Christ. Amen.

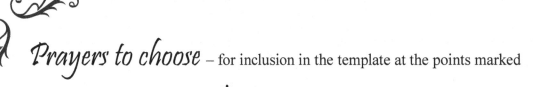

Prayers to choose – for inclusion in the template at the points marked

*

1. We invite You into our lives, to follow Your word and praise Your glory.

   In the words of Job: ***"... you can do all things ... {Lord] ... and ... no purpose of Yours can be thwarted,"*** (Job, Chapter 42) Thank You for Your great mercy towards us.

   We ask that this time of reflection, spent with You, will help us to understand Your call and know Your goodness. Help us, Lord, to put on the armour of Your love to enhance everything that we do.

   We serve You, trust in You and learn from You. We offer our prayers to You, today, as witnesses of Your loving kindness and mercy and to ask for Your guidance for the future. In praying to You, may we find the peace and rest that only You can give.

   We thank You for Your never-ending love for us and we surrender all we have to You: our hopes and skills, our need for help, our concerns, fears and worries and our compassion for other people.

   We praise You, thank You for Your mercy and look to You to guide us. Please give us strong wills to follow Your word and hope for the future.

   We seek Your guidance. We praise and thank You for the love You show to each one of us. We look to You to renew and refresh us in our appreciation of Your will and our hopes for the future.

   We praise You for the great mercy and love You show to us and ask You to provide us with all that is needed for us to carry forward Your word lovingly and knowingly.

   [Trinity Sunday] On this Trinity Sunday we come before You: God the Father Almighty, Christ our Saviour and the Holy Spirit of truth and love. We offer our praise and adoration, ask You to hold us near and submit our hopes and concerns to You for the future.

   [Harvest] We give thanks to You Lord for the harvest and its gifts of fruit, vegetables and flowers. Please help us to nurture another harvest: one of peace, love, kindness, forgiveness, mercy and enhanced understanding of Your will. We ask for this Lord so that we can do our part in producing a better world for the future.

[All Saints' Day / All Saints' Sunday] We thank You, Lord, for the powerful, shining examples of devotion and witness given to us by the Saints. We value the sharing of their faith with us through the ages. We praise You for the inspiration granted to us by their bravery and sacrifice.

[Remembrance Sunday] Lord, we pray for all who suffer and have suffered in the past through injury, displacement and death as a result of conflict, including people in the armed forces, civilians and refugees. Also, we pray for those who have been left behind and are saddened by loss. We are grateful for the bravery and cherish the memory of members of the armed forces who have fought for our freedom and lost their lives. Please help us, Lord, to rise above the agony of strife and to do our part in making a better world where fighting, injury and death are replaced by peace, love and harmony.

2. We thank You, Lord, for all of Your people with their differing cultures and environments in our world. We pray for their freedom and that conflict, poverty and persecution will be replaced by the growth of love and peace.

We trust in You, Lord, to help the people for whom we pray in their time of need. Please send Your love into the hearts of all who suffer, that they will receive the blessings of joy, peace and hope. [Words selected from Paul's Letter to the Romans (Chapters 5 and 15)]

In the words of Isaiah: ***"… [Help those, Lord] … who wait for … [You, that they may] … renew their strength … run and not be weary … walk and not faint,"*** (Isaiah, Chapter 40).

We trust in You, Lord to help us. We are Your children and ask for Your blessing. Give us hope that we will be saved and help us to work for good, for if You are for us, no-one can be against us. [Words selected from Paul's Letter to the Romans (Chapter 8)]

We know that Your peace will keep our hearts and minds safe in union with Christ Jesus. Lord, we ask for what we need, with humility and we thank You for what we have received in the past. [Words selected from Letter to the Philippians (Chapter 4)].

Lord, please help the nations of the world to show their love by their tolerance towards others, their will to preserve unity and their efforts to build for a peace that binds all of us together. [Words selected from Letter to the Ephesians (Chapter 4)]

We trust in You, Lord, to help the people for whom we pray in their time of need. Lord, please send Your love into the hearts of all who suffer, that they will receive the blessings of joy, peace and hope. [Words selected from Letter to the Romans (Chapters 5 and 15)]

3. Loving Lord Jesus, during your earthly ministry you healed the sick. We ask for your goodness and grace for those who are unwell and their families and friends, on our list in Church and throughout the world. Also, we ask for the gifts of wisdom and insight for the dedicated people who address their needs.

In the words of Isaiah: *"Comfort, O comfort … says [the Lord] … [I] … will feed … [my] … flock like a shepherd …[and] … gather the lambs in… [my] … arms*, (Isaiah, Chapter 40).

Please send Your great gift of love to those who carry the burden of suffering, Lord. You have told us, through St. Paul, that love is patient, kind and eternal and that it supersedes even faith and hope. Please help those who are unwell with their burdens, through Your great love. [Words selected from First Letter to the Corinthians (Chapter 13)]

4. Lord, You brought us to birth and in Your arms we die. Please comfort those who are in grief, embrace them with Your love and give them hope in a new life with You.

In our sorrow, when remembering those who have departed, we seek comfort from You, Lord. In the words of Isaiah: *"God is … [our] … salvation. … [We] … will trust and … not be afraid … [He]… is …[our] … strength …[and] … might."*

Our comfort is in You Lord for You have told us, in the words of St. Paul, that: *You have a house in heaven for us, … a home [that You have made] … which lasts for ever.* [Words selected from First Letter to the Corinthians (Chapters 15 and 16) and Second Letter to the Corinthians (Chapter 5)]

5. Lord, please make us one in heart and mind, as we seek to make our service kind, true, loving and pleasing in Your sight. We pray especially for Christians in the world who are suffering for their faith, Lord, and that You will give them the strength of will to continue with their faithful service.

In the words of Job: *"… you can do all things … {Lord] … and … no purpose of Yours can be thwarted,"* (Job, Chapter 42) Thank You for Your great mercy towards us.

We thank You, Lord, for the skills and compassion of people in our community, local Churches and the worldwide Church who work for others. Please grant Your kindness and help to them so that they are able to continue in their faith, regardless of the pressures placed upon them and the difficulty of their situations.

Lord Jesus, we thank you for showing us the way to treat others, with love and forgiveness in our hearts. Help us to play our part in furthering your word throughout the world.

Please help us, on our journey through this earthly life, to understand and carry forward Your word dutifully, dependably, lovingly and with a clear sense of conscience.

In the words of St. Paul: ***"We ask for courage, strength and alertness, Lord, in the face of our troubles so that we may do Your work with conviction and love. We can have these things, and carry our faith as a shield, only through Your mighty power. Help us to go as the Spirit leads us, for the benefit of all God's people – filling our minds with all that is good and deserving of Your praise."***
[Words blended together from: First Letter to the Corinthians (Chapter 16), Letter to the Ephesians (Chapter 6) and Letter to the Philippians (Chapter 4)]

In the words of Isaiah: ***"Wonderful Counsellor, Mighty God. Everlasting Father … [help us to] … grow continually, … [and give us] … peace … from this time onward and for evermore.*** (Isaiah, Chapter 9)

Merciful Father …

Printed in the United States
by Baker & Taylor Publisher Services